Multivariate Estimation for Operational Risk with Judicious Use of Extreme Value Theory_

Mahmoud El-Gamal†, Hulusi Inanoglu‡, and Mitch Stengel§

OCC Economics Working Paper 2006-3

November 21, 2006

Abstract

The Basel II Accord requires participating banks to quantify operational risk according to a matrix of business lines and event types. Proper modeling of univariate loss distributions and dependence structures across those categories of operational losses is critical for proper assessment of overall annual operational loss distributions. We illustrate our proposed methodology using Loss Data Collection Exercise 2004 (LDCE 2004) data on operational losses across five loss event types. We estimate a multivariate likelihood-based statistical model, which illustrates the benefits and risks of using extreme value theory (EVT) in modeling univariate tails of event type loss distributions. We find that abandoning EVT leads to unacceptably low estimates of risk capital requirements, while indiscriminate use of EVT to all data leads to unacceptably high ones. The judicious middle approach is to use EVT where dictated by data, and after separating clear outliers that need to be modeled via probabilistic scenario analysis. We illustrate all computational steps in estimation of marginal distributions and copula with an application to one bank's data (disguising magnitudes to ensure that bank's anonymity). The methods we use to overcome heretofore unexplored technical problems in estimation of codependence across risk types scales easily to larger models, encompassing not only operational, but also other types of risks.

_Disclaimer: The views herein are those of the authors, and do not necessarily represent the views of the Office of the Comptroller of the Currency (OCC).
Acknowledgments: We thank Patrick de Fontnouvelle, Nick Kiefer, Mike Carhill, Steve Strasser and seminar participants at the Federal Reserve Bank of Philadelphia and the OCC for many useful comments and suggestions. We would like also to thank Regina Villasmil for her research assistance.
†Professor of Economics and Statistics, Rice University, Department of Economics, MS 22, 6100 Main St., Houston, TX; Email: elgamal@rice.edu, Phone: (713) 348-6301
‡Senior Economist, OCC, Risk Analysis Division, 250 E. St. SW, Washington, DC; Email: hulusi.inanoglu@occ.treas.gov, Phone: (202) 874-5428
§Senior Expert, OCC, Modeling and Analysis, 250 E. St. SW, Washington, DC; Email: mitch.stengel@occ.treas.gov, Phone: (202) 874-5431

1 Introduction

Following the Basel II Accord's requirement that banks should quantify their operational risk exposure in a systematic statistical manner, the Basel Committee's Risk Management Group has found that banks allocated, on average, approximately 15 percent of their capital for operational risk, c.f. [20, p. 37]. Moreover, recent studies have found instances wherein the capital charges for operational risk exceed those for market risk, c.f. [6].

In this regard, the the Basel II Accord encourages banks to perform operational risk quantification, and to design risk management techniques, at the most appropriate "granular" level. More granular units of measure help better to identify risk factors, supporting risk management efforts and improving the measurement of operational risk for capital adequacy calculations.

The new Accord provided categories for various types of operational risks along two dimensions: event types (e.g., fraud vs. execution) as well as business lines (e.g., corporate finance vs. retail banking). To date, it appears that most banks have not conducted their statistical operational risk quantification exercises at this level of disaggregation. This is likely due, in part, to unavailability of data, but may also in part be due to unavailability of sophisticated and yet easily implementable statistical procedures for making full use of the "granular" approach.

In this paper, we aim to make two main statistical contributions that may assist banks in making full use of the disaggregation approach to operational risk quantification, with an eye to eventual development of appropriate risk management techniques beyond computation of capital charges. Toward that end, we focus on the modeling of codependence between operational risks in various categories. We illustrate the inadequacy of simple linear correlation frameworks, and propose and illustrate a simple procedure for modeling the full codependence between operational losses for different event types.

In this regard, we tackle a fundamental technical problem for estimation of codependence of operational losses: the asynchronicity of loss arrival processes. We solve this problem, and simplify the analysis considerably while maintaining granularity and sufficient estimation precision, by aggregating losses of each given category over a short period of time. That provides us with continuous distributions for losses in the different categories (event types in our case), for which the full dependence structure can be modeled through estimation of univariate marginal loss distributions for each category, together with estimation of an appropriate copula.

The estimated dependence structure, and resulting capital charge estimation, depend not only on the use of copula, but also on the choices of marginal loss distributions for losses in various categories. In this regard, preliminary studies to date (c.f. [10]) have cast doubt on the use of extreme value theory (EVT) to model "fat tails" of univariate loss distributions. Those studies have found that the use of EVT yields excessively and unreasonably large capital charges, while the use of thin-tailed distributions yields unreasonably small ones.

2

In our multivariate statistical analysis of operational losses for five event types, we compare our results from different techniques. The best alternative, it appears, is to consider three types of losses: (1) regular losses (for which many thin tailed distribution, such as lognormal or gamma, may be fitted), (2) extreme losses (for which a fat tailed distribution, in particular generalized Pareto, may be fitted), and (3) outliers (extremely rare and large losses that need to be modeled subjectively, perhaps using Bayesian methods for elicitation of beliefs from experts, c.f. [15, 16]). In our analysis, we use maximum likelihood estimation for the univariate loss distributions (including thresholds for EVT, where appropriate), as well as copula. Extension to full Bayesian inference, especially if few observations are available, is thus straightforward from our likelihood-based framework.

Thus, our proposed framework aims to satisfy the Basel II Accord's requirements by (1) conducting the analysis at a disaggregated level, (2) using formal statistical methods for estimation of multivariate distributions, allowing for very general codependence structures, and (3) allowing for "fat tails" of some loss distributions. The statistical framework for our analysis is discussed in Section 2. Specific parametric models that are used in our data analysis are discussed in Section 3. Results of our analysis of data from one bank (after disguising that bank's data to preserve its anonymity) are shown in Section 4, and Section 5 concludes the paper.

2 Statistical Framework

One of the most important aspects of the Basel II Accord's treatment of operational risk is the emphasis on recognizing the sources and categories of risks being quantified. Quantification of risks by source and category would then lend itself more easily to risk estimation, including the use of combined internal and relevant external data, and scenario analysis. It would also aid in risk management, by informing the design of diversification, insurance, or hedging mechanisms that target specific risk types and risk sources, integrating the effects of internal controls in risk quantification and measurement.

Section 2.1 will provide a brief summary of the regulatory framework that focuses on defining appropriate units of measurement to quantify operational losses at a disaggregated level. To determine a bank's regulatory capital charge for operational risk, we need to reaggregate estimated loss distributions across the various units of measurement to obtain an overall estimated operational loss distribution. This aggregation process requires the use of an appropriate model of the statistical dependence structure across our units of measurement. In Section 3, we shall discuss the generally accepted statistical methodology that we use in this paper: modeling the multivariate distribution of losses across units of measurement by first modeling the marginal distributions for each unit, and then estimating an appropriate copula function to measure codependence.

As we shall discuss in Section 2.2, the estimation of copula – or any other means of capturing codependence of losses across units of measurement – requires matching observed losses temporally. This requires the definition of a unit of time over which the analysis will be conducted. If we choose a fine unit of time, such as a day, we will need to use a frequency-and-severity framework for estimating the distribution of losses. However, with different numbers of losses across a unit of time, one would only be able to model the dependence structure for the frequency process, but not for severities (since the latter are not be matched). We present a solution to this problem by aggregating losses across a unit of time (weekly) that is sufficiently coarse to avoid the problem of very small numbers of losses in any period, while being sufficiently fine to give us a sufficiently large data sample for analysis.

2.1 Unit of Measurement:

The Basel II Accord requires thinking about operational risk by units of measurement, commonly labeled categories, classes or cells. The latter terminology comes from envisioning a table of possible categories of loss events (event types) in different banking operations (business lines). As summarized in Table 1, the new Accord listed four sources of operational risk: people, processes, systems, and external. However, the sources are used mainly as heuristics for thinking of the categories of operational losses that a bank may experience. Those categories were broken into seven event types within each of eight business lines, as shown in Table 1. Each combination of event type and business line is then viewed as a "cell" in a matrix of disaggregated operational losses.

Table 1: Basel II Operational Risk Factors, Event Types, and Business Lines

Factors (Risk sources)	Event Types (Classification of risk types)	Business Lines (Refinement)
1. People 2. Processes 3. Systems 4. External	1. Internal fraud 2. External fraud 3. Empl. practices and workplace safety 4. Clients, products and business practices 5. Damage to physical assets 6. Business disruption and system failures 7. Exec. delivery and process management	1. Corporate finance 2. Trading and sales 3. Retail banking 4. Commercial banking 5. Payment and settlements 6. Agency services 7. Asset management 8. Retail brokerage

Of course, different event types and business lines may have varying significance for different banks. For instance, a processing bank would have operational risks dominated in

4

the three non-credit related business lines 5,6 and 7, c.f. [7]. Focusing on the relevant cells for each bank would help banks and regulators in determining the level of operational risk exposure and proper measures to manage it. Thus, we would like – ideally – to perform the analysis at the most granular level possible, using the matrix of event types and business lines as a point of departure. It is in this regard that Basel II states in paragraph 666(b): "The bank's internal operational risk measurement system must be closely integrated into the day-to-day risk management processes of the bank. Its output must be an integral part of the process of monitoring and controlling the bank's operational risk profile." In other words, if risk measurement takes place at a coarse level, it will be mainly a compliance exercise. Hence, for operational risk measurement to be relevant to how the bank is actually run, it needs to take place at a more granular level.

Note, however, that all banks can disaggregate their operational losses based on event types, but they need not be bound by conducting the analysis for the eight listed business lines, since they may not practice in those lines, or they may practice in areas that cannot be classified according to the standard list. In fact, for most banks in LDCE 2004, there were no reported losses in certain business lines, and many event-type/business-line cells had no reported losses for significant portions of the dataset. This justifies our focus on event types for the remainder of this paper, whereby we shall conduct the analysis on losses by event type, aggregated across business lines. In addition, event type segregation enables banks to see the root causes of losses while segregation by only business lines does not. By event type segregation, banks can link the losses with risk sources shown in Table 1, thus informing them regarding how to manage the risk. On the other hand, if the units of measurement are analyzed only by business line, the comingling of losses from different sources would make the risk management exercise more difficult. We are aware that in the event of lack of data, some banks prefer first disaggregation by business lines, since business lines thus would have their own capital estimates directly. Ultimately, the method we develop is applicable to both event type and business line disaggregation. To illustrate our method, we chose to start with analysis by event type in order to draw attention to its potential role in integration of risk measurement and management.

2.2 Dependence structure and a technical problem

Another major advantage of disaggregating operational losses by category is the resulting ability to estimate the dependence structure across those loss categories (for which we shall focus on event types, as discussed previously). One can easily see how codependence across loss types can be driven by the primary risk sources that contribute to those losses. For instance, the risk source "people" contributes mainly to event types 1, 3 and 7, "processes" contribute primarily to event types 4 and 7, "systems" contribute mainly to event type 6, and "external" contributes mainly to event types 2 and 5.

It would be excessively pessimistic to compute operational risk capital by computing the 99.9% value at risk (VaR) for each event type, and then to add those up. That would be assuming perfect correlation across the various operational loss types. Instead, one can estimate a dependence structure across the loss types, and use the estimated joint distribution of operational losses to simulate or calculate analytically the 99.9% aggregate annual VaR to obtain the regulatory capital charge. The difference between the capital charge assuming perfect correlation and that using an estimated dependence structure is commonly called a "diversification effect" (not all extreme losses are likely to occur at the same time). Basel II recognizes such diversification effects, but requires disclosure of the statistical methods used to estimate them (Basel II paragraph 669(d)), for which it provides very little guidance at this stage.

As we shall discuss in Section 3, the generally accepted paradigm for estimation of the joint distribution of losses is estimation of marginal distributions for various loss types, and then using those estimated marginals to estimate a copula distribution, which completes the characterization of a joint distribution. We shall leave technical details of this procedure for Section 3, and operational details of how we implement it for Section 4. In this section, we need to discuss a conceptual problem that complicates the implementation of this standard procedure, which is borrowed from market risk quantification frameworks, for operational risk measurement.

The model of choice in risk management in recent years has been the loss distribution approach (LDA), adopted from the insurance industry. The LDA framework breaks the distribution of losses into two components: a discrete distribution for frequency of loss occurrence, and a continuous distribution for severity of loss conditional on its occurrence. Mathematically, the aggregate loss (AL) may be written as:

$$AL = \sum_{n=1}^{N} X_n = X_1 + ... + X_N$$

where N is a random number measuring frequency of losses and X_n are loss severities. While this is a useful model for univariate loss distributions, it is not at all clear how one would estimate codependence for multivariate losses within this framework.

One can allow for codependence of frequencies of loss occurrences per time unit (daily, weekly, etc.) by estimating a multivariate discrete distribution for frequencies (e.g. negative multinomial, also known as multivariate negative binomial).[1] However, codependence of severities is all but impossible to estimate: Imagine if we had no losses of one type, and two of another in one period, and the opposite in another, how would one even calculate a simple correlation of loss magnitudes? In fact unless losses are matched together in some manner, it appears impossible to estimate a joint distribution of their magnitudes, either directly with a multivariate parametric model, or indirectly by estimating marginal distributions and copula.

---

[1]For instance, [13, 19] correlate frequencies of loss occurrence, but not severities. This approach has very limited usefulness, since codependence of loss severities (especially for large losses, as we shall discuss in Section 4) is much more important than codependence of loss occurrences. Moreover, most multivariate discrete distributions put limits on permissible codependence, (c.f. [14]).

One solution to overcome the synchronization problem of operational losses is to aggregate losses of each type over a unit of time. In this manner, aggregate losses of each type for that unit of time are synchronized with aggregate losses of each other type for the same unit, and a joint distribution for those losses can be estimated with a multivariate distribution directly or indirectly. As discussed in Section 4, aggregating the daily data reported in LDCE 2004 at the weekly level provided us with sufficient numbers of observations for each loss type (196 observations over the 45-month sample period), while avoiding the technical problem of asynchronicity of losses.[2]

3 Statistical Methods

Having ruled out the use of actuarial loss distribution methods, our multivariate statistical modeling of the joint distribution of losses across various event types requires only two components: estimation of univariate loss distributions, and estimation of a copula function. This follows from the well known Sklar's theorem, c.f. [21, 18], which states that any multivariate distribution function $F \colon \mathbb{R}^d \to [0, 1]$ can be fully characterized by its margin CDFs $F_1, ..., F_d$ (each $F_i \colon \mathbb{R} \to [0, 1]$, $i = 1, \ldots, d$) and copula function $C_F \colon [0, 1]^d \to [0, 1]$, whereby C_F is a multivariate CDF with uniform margins on [0,1] . Thus,

$$F(\mathbf{x}) = C_F\big(F_1(x_1), ..., F_d(x_d)\big), \quad \mathbf{x} \in \mathbb{R}^d$$

The CDF C_F is called a copula for F. If the margins F_i, $i = 1, \ldots, d$, are all continuous, the copula C_F is uniquely defined by:

$$C_F(\mathbf{u}) = F\big(F_1^{-1}(u_1), ..., F_d^{-1}(u_d)\big), \quad \mathbf{u} \in [0, 1]^d$$

In our analysis, we shall use the t-copula, which has been most preferred in risk management, since it allows for fat tails and simultaneous large observations with small degrees of freedom, while nesting Gaussian-like thin tails for large degrees of freedom (c.f. [12] and [8]). The t-copula has two parameters: degrees of freedom ν, and (Spearman) correlation matrix P. It is defined by:

$$C_{\nu,P}^t(\mathbf{u}) = \mathbf{t}_{\nu,P}(t_\nu^{-1}(u_1), ..., t_\nu^{-1}(u_d)), \quad \mathbf{u} \in [0, 1]^d,$$

where $t_\nu(.)$ is univariate student t cdf with ν degrees of freedom, and $\mathbf{t}_{\nu,P}(.)$ is the multivariate density student t cdf with ν degrees of freedom and Spearman correlation matrix P, c.f. [18, p.151]. Thus, fatter tails and higher tail dependence can be captured with low values of ν, and vice versa.

It thus remains to define our choice of univariate marginal distributions of operational losses for various event types. Previous studies have shown that if a single distribution

---

[2]Note that the same considerations apply equally to multivariate credit risk measurement.

7

is fitted to operational losses, capital charge estimates depend critically on the choice of distribution, c.f. [10]. On the other hand, if one distribution is fitted to loss severities up to some threshold, and extreme value theory (EVT) is invoked to fit a generalized Pareto distribution to exceedances above that threshold, then the choice of the first distribution is relatively immaterial, c.f. [6], except to the extent that it may influence threshold choice. In this regard, the relevant component of extreme value theory is the result that the distribution of exceedances above a threshold becomes arbitrarily well approximated by the GPD as threshold value goes to infinity, c.f. [11] and [1]. The GPD cdf for exceedances x (equal to observed value less threshold) is defined by two parameters τ and γ as follows:

$$
GPD_{\gamma,\tau}(x) = \begin{cases} 1 - (1 + \frac{\gamma x}{\tau})^{-1/\gamma} & \text{if } \gamma \neq 0, \\ \\ 1 - \exp(-x/\tau) & \text{if } \gamma = 0, \end{cases}
$$

where τ and γ are scale and shape parameters, respectively. For $\gamma > 0$, the distribution is heavy tailed (i.e. the density value declines slower than exponential), and tail heaviness increases with γ.

The final remaining issue is choice of the threshold. That choice is subject to a classical bias-variance tradeoff: As threshold value rises, the GPD approximation becomes more accurate and bias is reduced in estimates of γ and τ. However, that is obtained at the expense of higher variance of those estimates, as the number of observations above the threshold declines. Conversely, as the threshold declines, estimation variance falls, but at the expense of rising bias (unless the distribution is in fact GPD). Various methods have been devised to approach optimality in this bias-variance tradeoff, including ocular inspection of estimates of γ for various threshold values, as well as more formal statistical procedures, c.f. [5]. As explained in Section 4, we decided to invoke the likelihood principle by maximizing overall likelihood for the dataset, using a lognormal distribution fit for losses below the threshold and GPD distribution fit for exceedances above that threshold. This approach was also used in Bayesian univariate analysis of loss distributions, e.g. [2]. See subsection 4.3 for more details on our procedure to maximize likelihood over all parameters, including the threshold choice.

4   Data Analysis and Results

We now turn to the specific empirical investigation of operational risk in one of the participating banks in LDCE 2004, c.f. [17]. We have already discussed one of the intrinsic data limitations in Section 2, namely that operational losses of different types are not synchronized, and hence the dependence structure of their magnitudes cannot be modeled directly in the collected data. As discussed in that section, we solve that technical problem by aggregating losses of each type at the weekly level. This gives us 196 observations for each cell in the operational risk categories matrix, each cell corresponding to a particular business line and event type.

However, two data limitations force us also to limit the number of units of measurement. The first limitation forces us to exclude event types 5 (damage to physical assets) and 6 (business disruptions and system failures). The number of reported losses in those two event types are very small relative to the other five. Fortunately, the dollar magnitudes of losses in those event types are also very small relative to losses of other types (e.g., fraud or legal losses), and hence we can exclude those statistically problematic event types 5 and 6 from the analysis without affecting the estimated distribution of overall operational losses substantially.

The second data limitation hinders our ability to perform the analysis at the level of each cell in the risk categories matrix (i.e., by event types for each business line). As discussed previously, many of the cells are very sparsely populated both at the daily level, and also after aggregation to the weekly level. Consequently, we have decided to conduct our analysis for aggregated weekly losses over all business lines for each of the remaining five event types: ET1 (internal fraud), ET2 (external fraud), ET3 (employment practices and workplace safety), ET4 (clients, products, and business practices) and ET7 (execution, delivery and process management). This choice of aggregation also has the advantage of being robust, since all banks report losses for the same event types, but each defines its own relevant list of business lines.

4.1 Exploratory Data Analysis

Thus, our departure point for data analysis is the data set comprised of 196 weekly sums of operational losses for each of five event types, aggregated over all business lines. A scatter plot of this raw series is shown in Figure 1. The bottom triangular part of the figure shows scatter plots of weekly loss magnitudes for each pair of event types. The top part of the figure shows linear correlations between each pair. The event types for each cell in the upper and lower triangles is identified by the diagonal labels. We can clearly see that few observations can dominate the linear correlation measure of codependence of those series. For instance, the largest linear correlation (0.47) is that between event types 2 and 3. However, it is clear from the scatter plot of those two types that one week with large losses in both event types is driving that high correlation. In later analyses in this section, we shall see correlation scatter plots corresponding to Spearman correlations, which we use in copula estimation, and which are robust to such high leverage observations.

The correlation structure for the five event types suggests that there is statistically significant correlation between losses. In Table 2, we report the results of pairwise tests of uncorrelatedness of the event type losses.

For now, we present another graphical representation of the codependence structure of the raw data to emphasize the importance of thinking about codependence of extreme events, and not only about linear correlation.

9

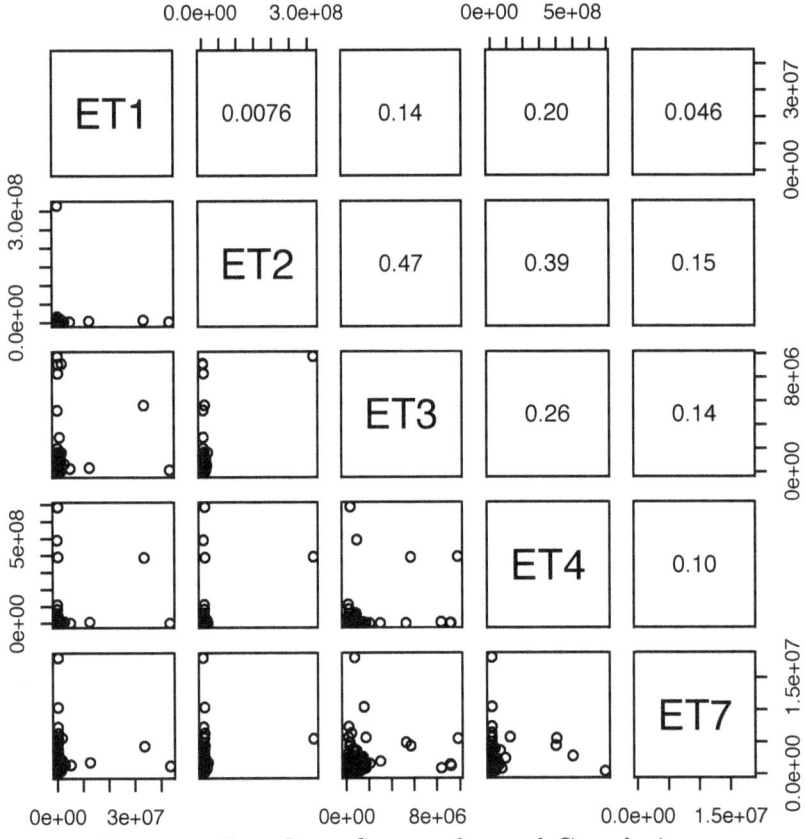

Figure 1: Raw Data Scatterplot and Correlations

Table 2: Pearson's Product-moment Correlations and Tests of Uncorrelatedness

Event Types	Pearson Corr.	t-statistic	d.f.	p-value
E1, E2	-0.008	-0.106	194	0.915
E1, E3	0.139	1.952	194	0.052
E1, E4	0.204	2.900	194	0.004
E1, E7	0.046	0.648	194	0.518
E2, E3	0.469	7.389	194	4 E-12
E2, E4	0.385	5.814	194	2 E-08
E2, E7	0.155	2.179	194	0.031
E3, E4	0.259	3.733	194	0.0002
E3, E7	0.143	2.014	194	0.045
E4, E7	0.103	1.446	194	0.150

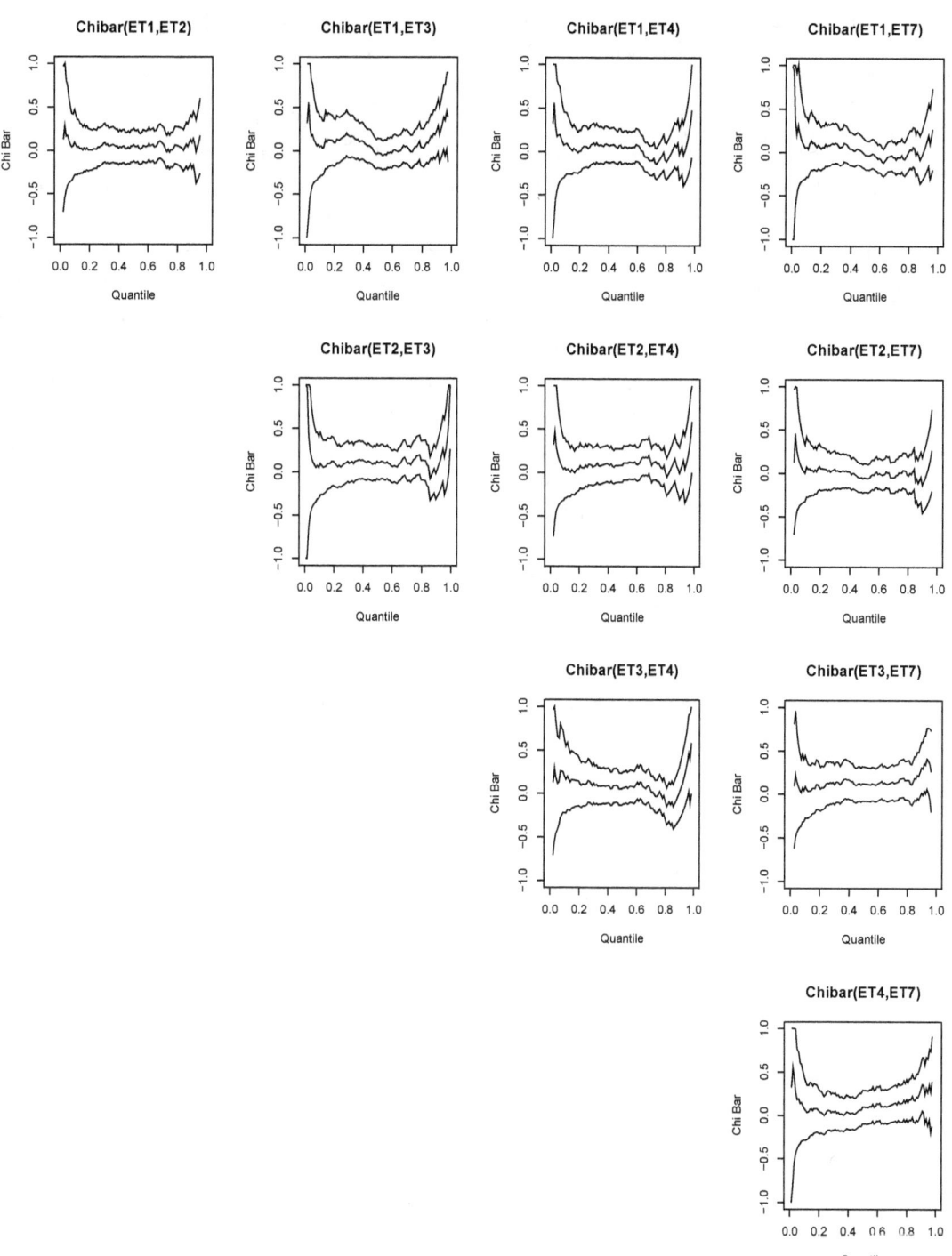

Figure 2: Dependence Structure at Various Quantiles

In Figure 2, we show $\bar{\chi}$ plots for the bivariate samples of each pair of event types. The function $\bar{\chi}(q) \in [-1, 1]$ is a measure of codependence calculated at each quantile q as follows, c.f. [3, 4]:

$$\bar{\chi}(q) = \frac{2\log(1 - q)}{\log(\Pr\{F_X(x) > q, F_Y(y) > q\})} - 1,$$

where F_X and F_Y are the marginal distribution functions for variables X and Y respectively. Hence $\bar{\chi}(q)$ measures the tendency for X to exceed the quantile q at the same time that Y exceeds q. Looking at the $\bar{\chi}$ plot for event types ET2 and ET3, we can see that there is virtually no codependence at most quantiles, with the notable exception of the very highest 99th percentile, as expected from our visual inspection of the scatter plots in Figure 1. Similar patterns can be seen for event pairs (ET2, ET4) and (ET3, ET4).

In figure 3, we perform one final visual inspection of the data to assess the need for employing extreme value theory methods. In that figure, we show mean excess and exponential-quantile-quantile plots (QQ-plots) for the five event types. The upward sloping mean excesses and concave QQ-plots suggest the need for EVT treatment, at least for event types 2, 4, and 7, as we shall see in our likelihood-based statistical analysis below.

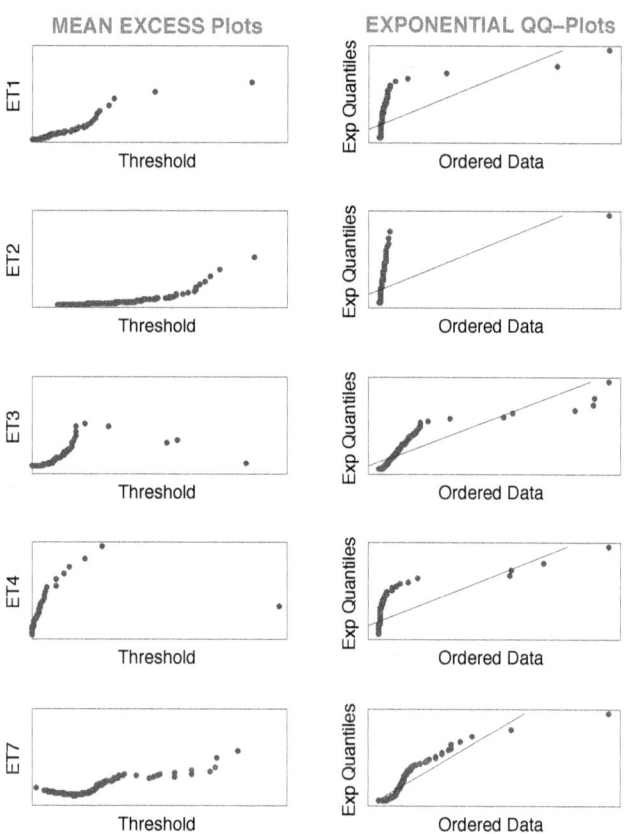

Figure 3: Are operational losses heavy tailed?

4.2 Data Analysis without Extreme Value Theory

We begin our analysis by ignoring the fat tails of operational loss distributions – perhaps a straw-man model given the clear fat tails shown in Figure 3, but a good benchmark nonetheless. In Figures 4-8, we show density plots and QQ-plots for fitted lognormal distributions of all five series. For event types 1 and 3, we also plot the marginal likelihood function over thresholds, which we shall discuss in detail in subsection 4.3. The density and QQ-plots show good fits of the lognormal distribution to the bulk of loss observations, but also the distribution's inability to capture very large observed losses.

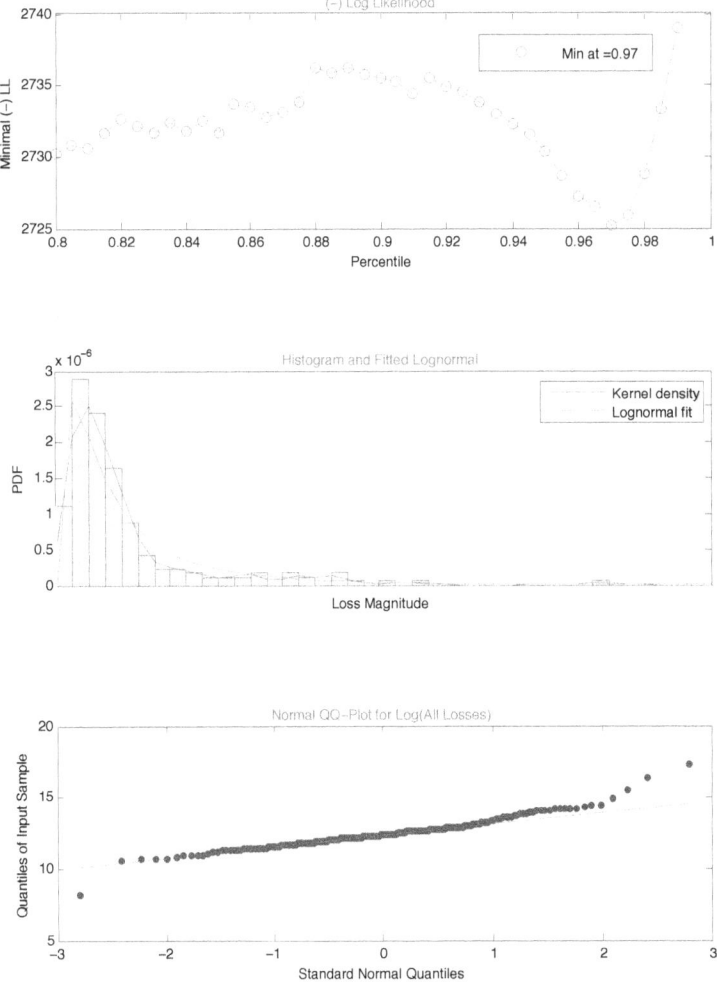

Figure 4: Lognormal Fit for Event Type 1

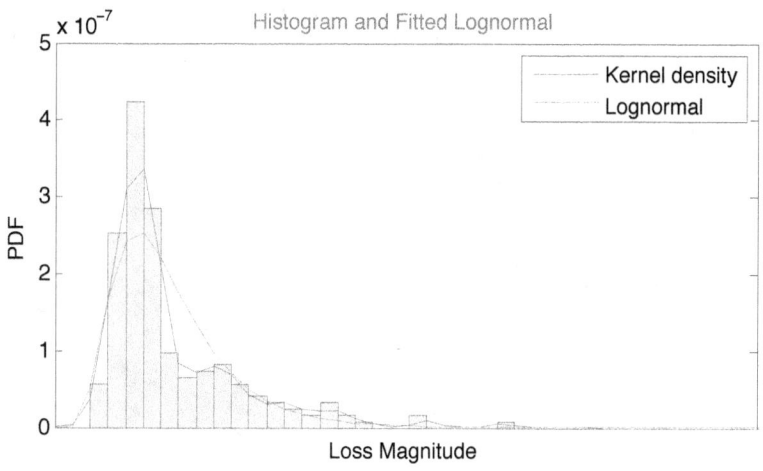

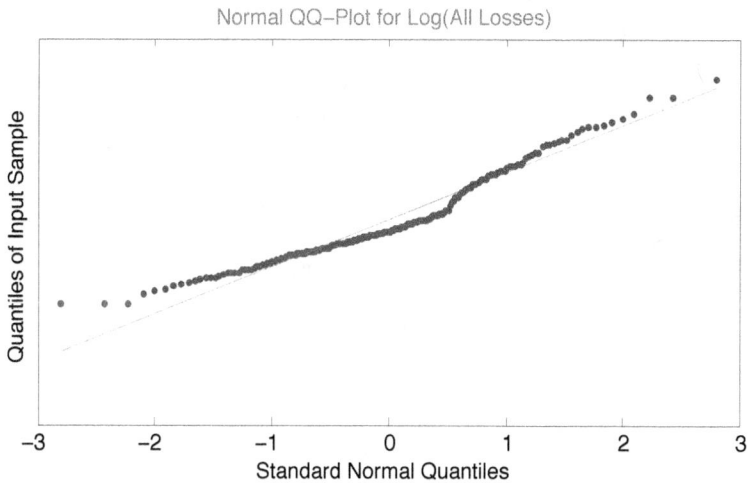

Figure 5: Lognormal Fit for Event Type 2

15

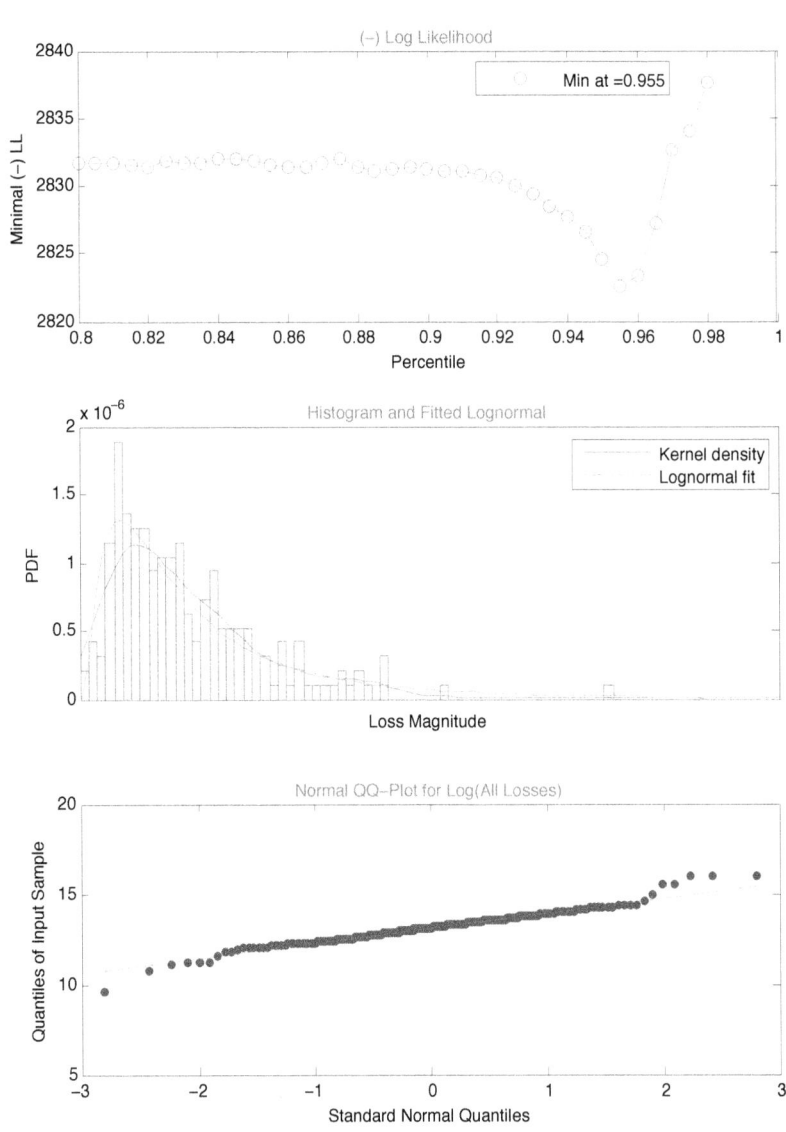

Figure 6: Lognormal Fit for Event Type 3

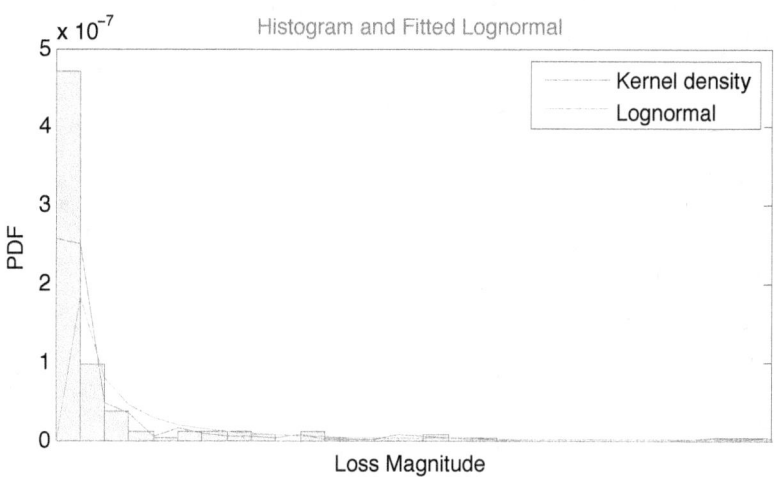

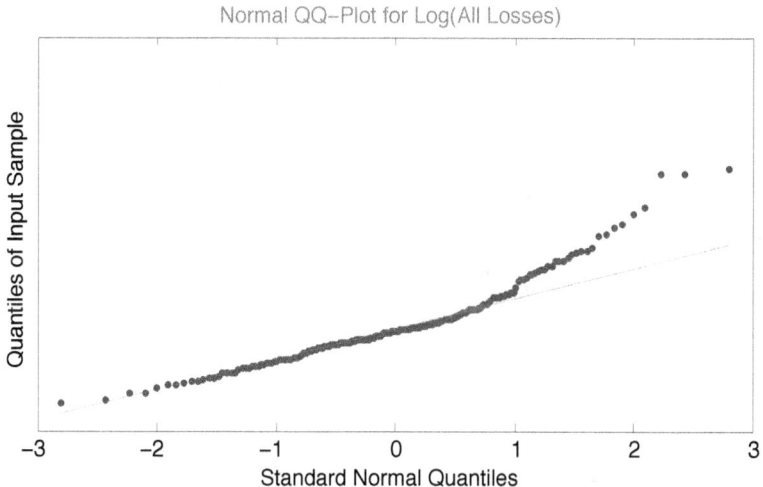

Figure 7: Lognormal Fit for Event Type 4

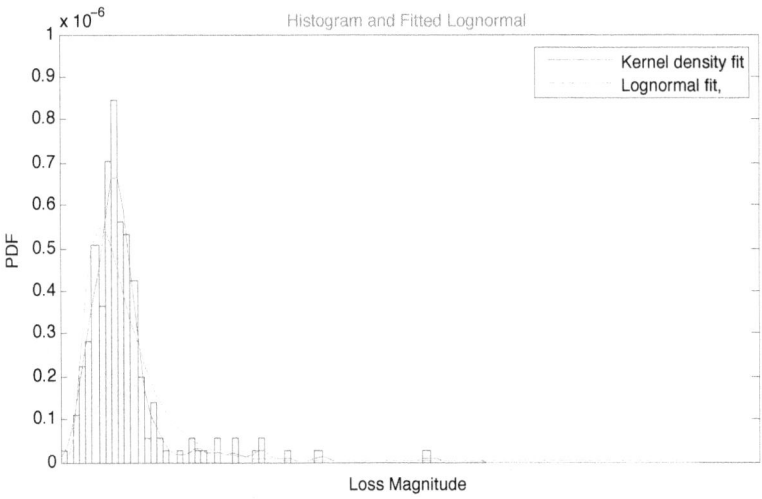

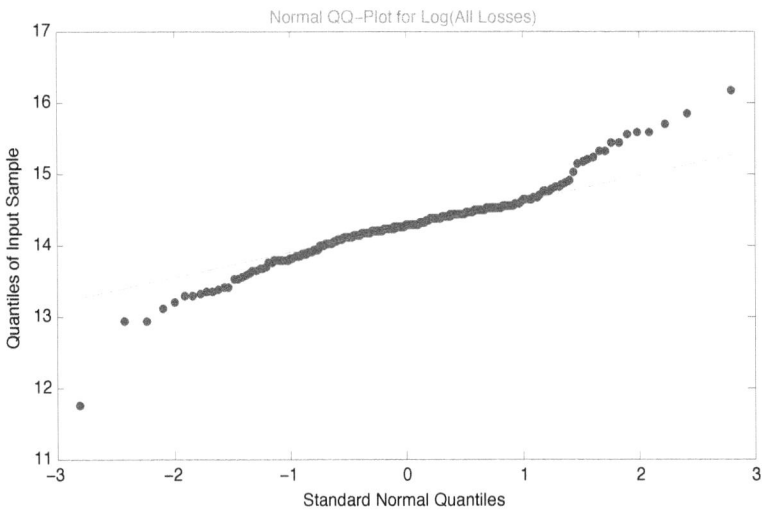

Figure 8: Lognormal Fit for Event Type 7

Since the lognormal density model fits most observations very well, as seen in Figures 4-8, we shall continue to use that model with the addition of the generalized Pareto density (GPD) model for "tail" losses beyond some threshold, as discussed in Section 3. For now, we proceed with the analysis without any allowance for "fat tails". In Figure 9, we show a scatter plot of the data transformed through the estimated lognormal CDF marginals for the five event types. The correlations shown in the upper triangle part of the Figure correspond to the Spearman correlations between those variables, equal to $\rho_S(x_1, x_2) = \rho(F_1(x_1), F_2(x_2))$, under the lognormal model for marginal CDFs. Comparing those correlations to the linear correlations (especially, e.g. for the pair ET2 and ET3) in Figure 1 illustrates two important points: (1) that linear correlation can be very misleading in the presence of high leverage data points of simultaneous large losses, and (2) that the lognormal model may in fact be excessively indifferent to such simultaneous tail events.

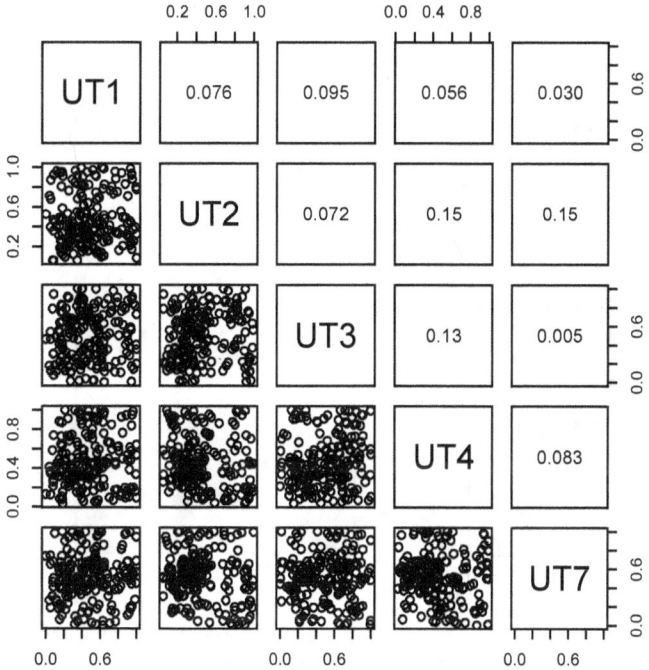

Figure 9: Transformed Data Scatterplot and Correlations: All Lognormal Model

Using the transformed data in Figure 9, we fit a 5-dimensional t-copula, which we then use to simulate 100,000 random years, each containing 52 random weekly losses from the estimated lognormal marginal distributions and t-copula with the shown Spearman correlations. The resulting distribution of annual operational losses is shown in Figure 10.

19

To address the magnitudes of estimated annual loss percentiles, while ensuring the bank's anonymity, we have multiplied (or divided) annual loss simulations by a scalar factor, so that $1 billion corresponds to the bank's own internal estimate of operational loss capital for 2004 (calculated as VaR at the 99.9% level). By comparison to that number, it is clear that the simulated $VaR_{99.9\%}$ of $327 million shown in Figure 10 is very low. Of course, that is not surprising, as the estimated lognormal marginal distributions have thin tails, and therefore undersample in the region of high losses of all types. Indeed, due to

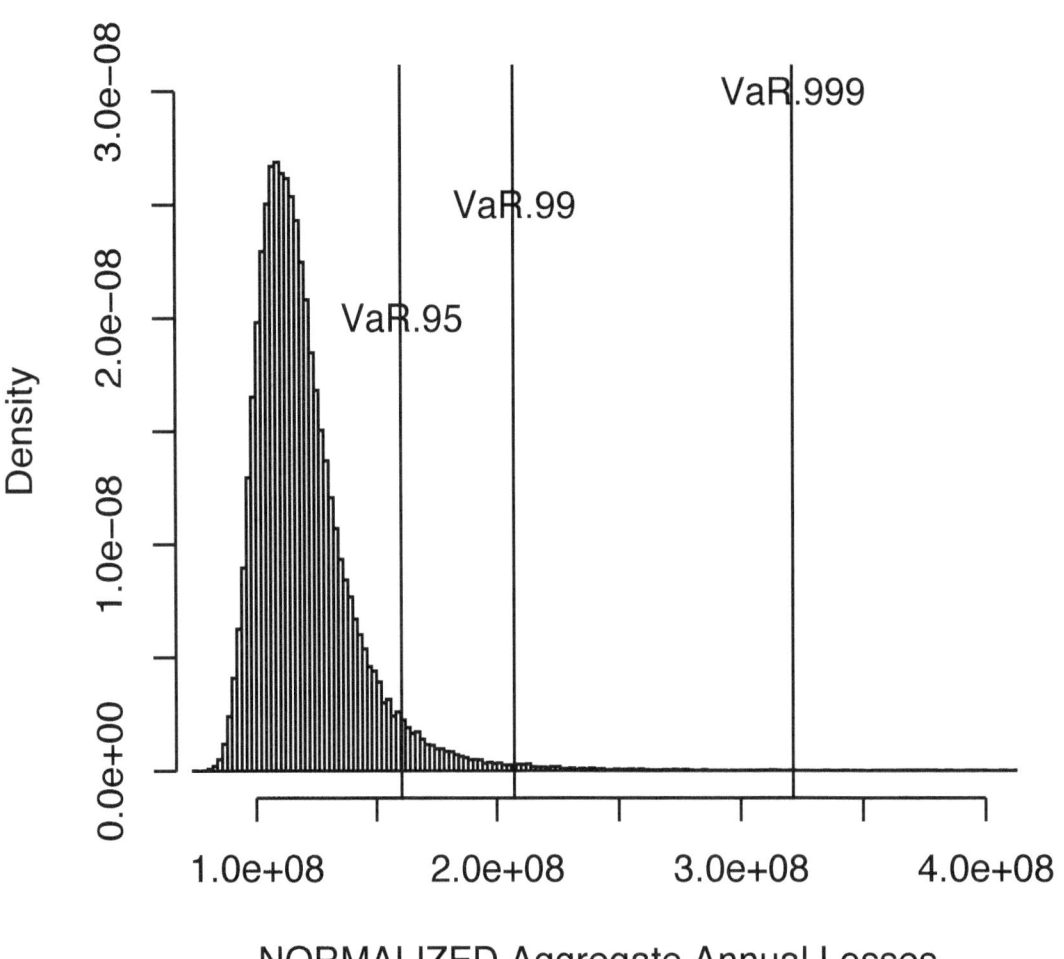

Figure 10: The Bottom Line Distribution– All Lognormal Model

4.3 Lognormal Bodies and GPD Tails

The next model we consider has been – to date – the workhorse of risk measurement estimation: a mixture of lognormal distribution (fitted for small or moderate losses) and generalized Pareto distribution (fitted for large or extreme losses), c.f. [9]. Instead of using ad hoc ocular methods, such as inspection of Hill plots with various excluded exceedances to determine the threshold beyond which the GPD model is fit, we use a full maximum likelihood procedure with five parameters (log-mean and log-standard deviation for the lognormal distribution, a quantile for the threshold, and shape and dispersion parameters for the GPD distribution). This is also the combined likelihood function used in [2].

Since the likelihood function is not smooth in the threshold percentile (it is asymptotically, but for finite samples, it jumps at percentiles corresponding to adding or removing an observation from the subsample), we perform a grid search on the threshold quantile. For each point on that grid, we maximize the overall likelihood function using the lognormal density up to the corresponding threshold, and the normalized GPD density for exceedances (where the normalization is 1 less the lognormal CDF of the threshold, so that the likelihood function integrates to unity).

In other words, for each quantile λ and corresponding threshold T_λ, the likelihood function at observation x is:

$$
L(x|\mu,\sigma,\lambda,\gamma,\tau) =
\begin{cases}
f_{LN}(x|\mu,\sigma) & \text{if } x \leq T_\lambda, \\
(1 - F_{LN}(T_\lambda|\mu,\sigma)) \times f_{GPD}(x - T_\lambda|\gamma,\tau) & \text{if } x > T_\lambda,
\end{cases}
$$

where $f_{LN}(.|.)$ and $F_{LN}(.|.)$ are, respectively, the lognormal pdf and cdf evaluated at the stated data point and parameter values, and f_{GPD} is the pdf of the generalized Pareto cdf discussed in Section 3.

As customary, we maximize likelihood by minimizing negative log likelihood. Negative log likelihood for each λ is $nll(\mathbf{x}|\mu,\sigma,\lambda,\gamma,\tau) = -\sum_{i=1}^{n} \log L(x_i|\mu,\sigma,\lambda,\gamma,\tau)$, which we minimize over (μ,σ,γ,τ), and then choose the overall minimum over $(\mu,\sigma,\lambda,\gamma,\tau)$. For event types 1 and 3, the marginal negative log likelihood at each threshold quantile (i.e., the minimized negative log likelihood value over μ, σ, γ, and τ with that threshold quantile fixed) are shown at the top of Figures 4 and 6, respectively. For event types 2, 4, and 7, those marginal negative log likelihood functions are shown at the tops of Figures 11, 12, and 13, respectively.

Given the extremely high threshold quantiles (above 95%) at which negative log likelihood is minimized for event types 1 and 3, there are insufficient numbers of exceedances to fit GPD models for those event types (and if we fit GPD models to those few observations, we obtain $\hat{\gamma} < 0$, indicating thin tails). Hence, we maintain the lognormal distribution for the entire samples of those two event types. For event types 2, 4, and 7, the maximum likelihood estimates of threshold quantiles are 20%, 83.5%, and 28%, respectively (for anonymity purposes, we do not report actual threshold dollar values, lest the bank be easily identified). In other words, the likelihood function chooses fat tailed distributions for the bulk of types 2 and 7 operational losses. Interestingly, those two types of operational losses are similar to losses in the insurance industry, where the entire distribution above a relatively-low threshold (corresponding to policy deductible) is commonly modeled by fat-tailed distributions: Event type 2 is external fraud, which is one of the major sources of risk to insurance companies, and event type 7 relates to internal processes which are similar across various financial institutions.

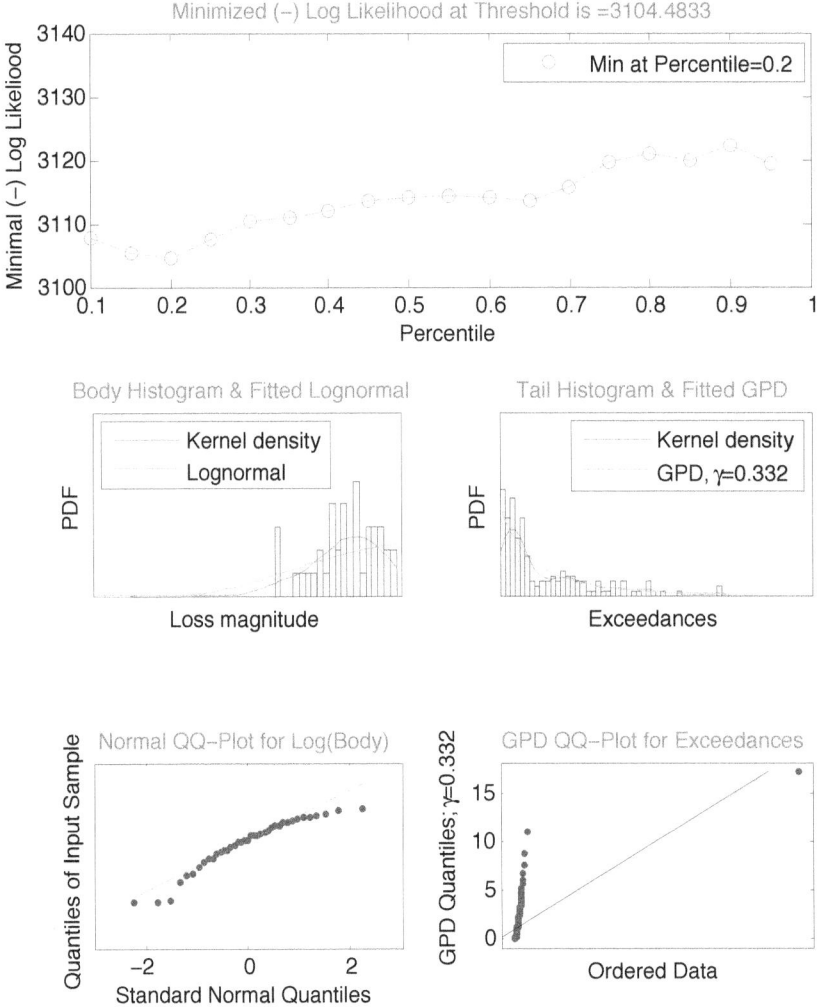

Figure 11: Lognormal Body & GPD Tail Fit for Event Type 2

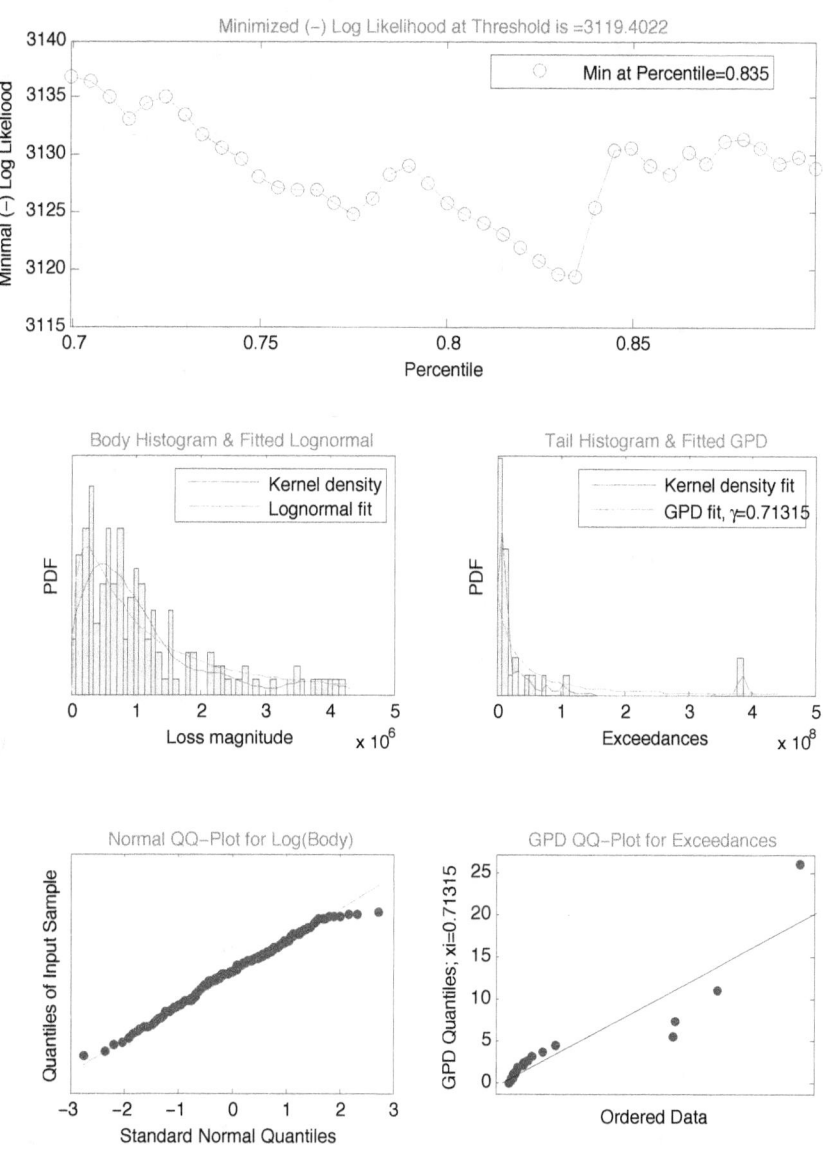

Figure 12: Lognormal Body & GPD Tail Fit for Event Type 4

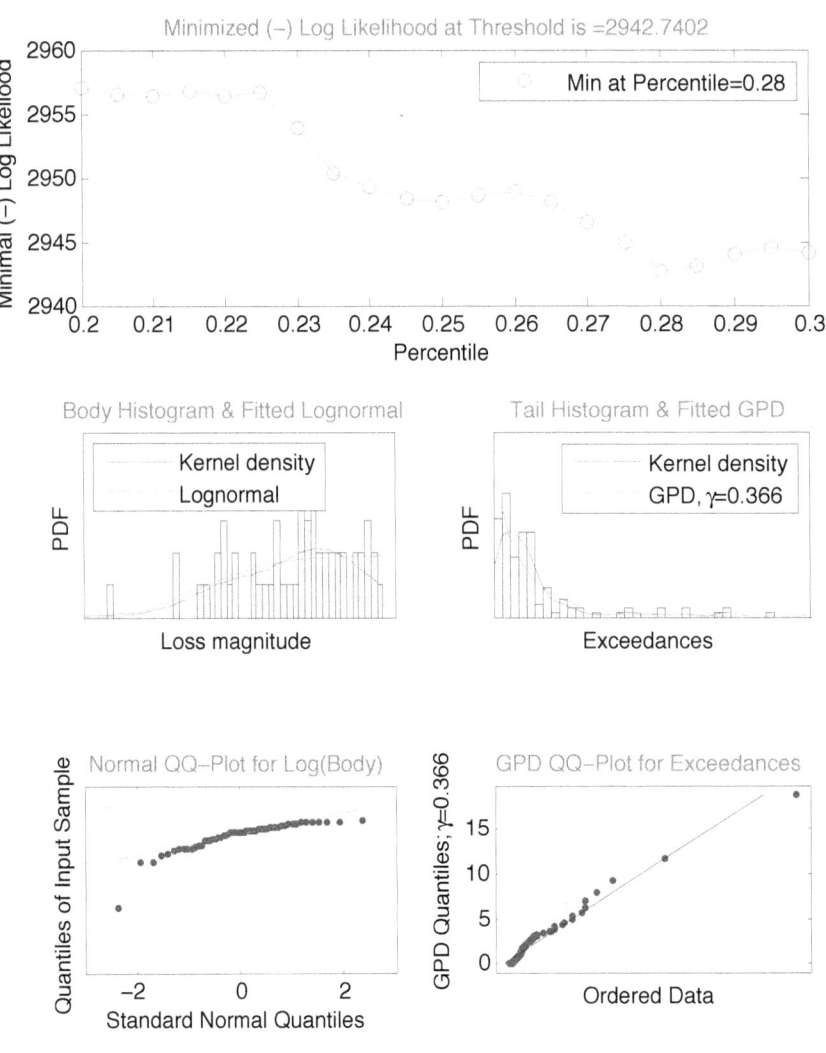

Figure 13: Lognormal Body & GPD Tail Fit for Event Type 7

Figure 14 contains a scatter plot and Spearman correlations corresponding to the margins modeled by mixtures of lognormals and GPDs. In comparison to Figures 1 and 9, we can see that the significant correlations (e.g. between types 2 and 4) are once again restored once simultaneous tail events are recognized. On the other hand, the correlation between event types 2 and 3 is now somewhere between the very high value of the linear correlation in Figure 1 and the extremely low Spearman correlation of Figure 9. That is in large part driven by the fact that we do not allow for a fat tail in type 3, since the likelihood function favors modeling the overwhelming majority of observations under the lognormal distribution. We shall return to this issue with more insights in the next subsection, when we allow for excluding outliers in the main statistical analysis.

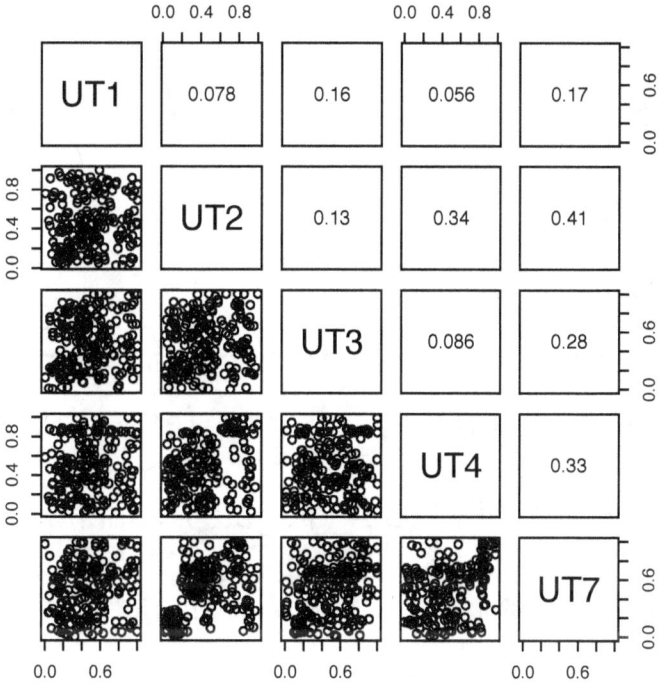

Figure 14: Scatterplot and Correlations: Lognormal Bodies & GPD Tails

We now proceed to simulate random sets of 52 weeks for 100,000 hypothetical years, using the estimated weekly distributions of the five types and a fitted t-copula using the Spearman correlations based on those marginal estimates. For this model, the estimated t-copula has only 5 degrees of freedom, thus accommodating fat tails and simultaneous large loss occurrences. The resulting distribution of annual operational risk losses (aggregated across all five event types) is shown in Figure 15. In this Figure, we have also normalized the annual losses so that \$1 billion corresponds to this bank's own internal estimate of the annual losses' $VaR_{99.9\%}$ for 2004. A $VaR_{99.9\%}$ of \$28.407 billion is clearly excessive.

25

Histogram of Simulated Annual Losses with VaR

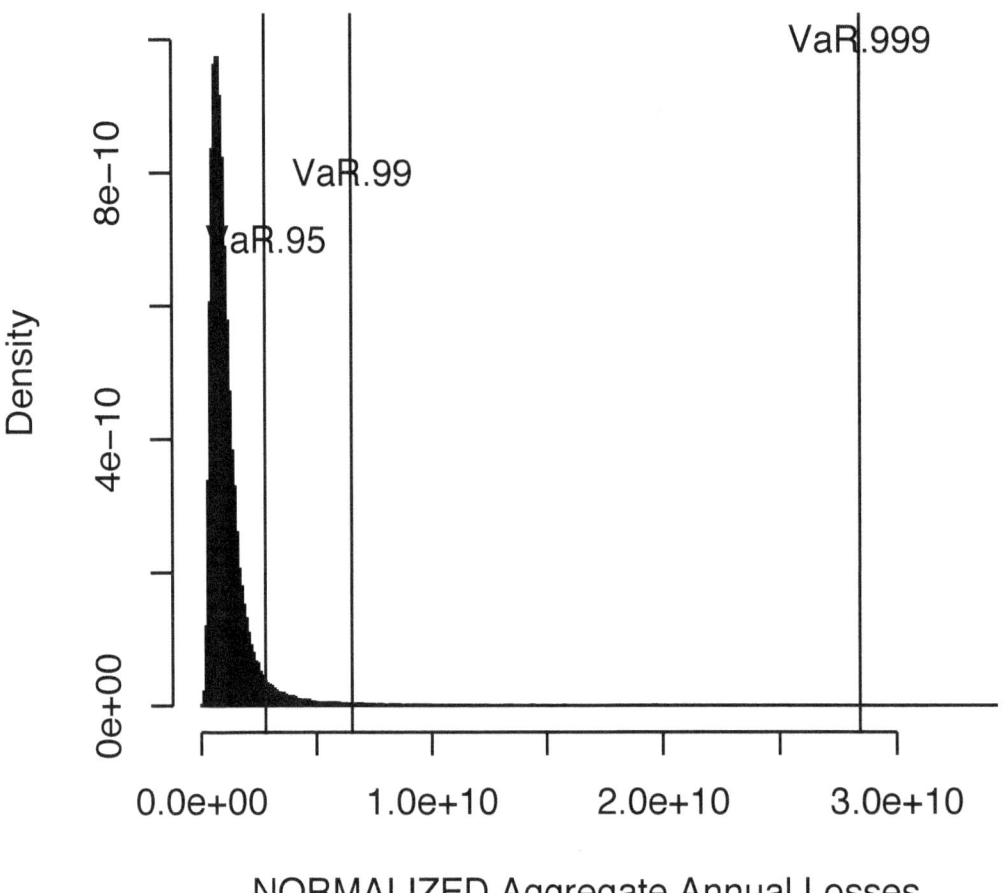

Figure 15: The Bottom Line: Lognormal Bodies & GPD Tails

We suspect that this extremely high VaR figure stems from the existence of abnormally high losses for some event types. In four of our 196 weeks, we observed such "outliers," which reached as high as 7.7 log-standard deviations above the log-mean of weekly losses for two event types. Hence, our final analysis will be conducted excluding those four "outlier" weeks, for which we recommend the use of probabilistic models of rare events, as suggested in [15, 16]. Note, moreover, that the dependence structure in our data is not adversely affected by excluding those four outlier weeks, as shown in Figure 16 (see, for instance, the continued co-dependence at high quantiles for ET2 with ET3 and ET4).

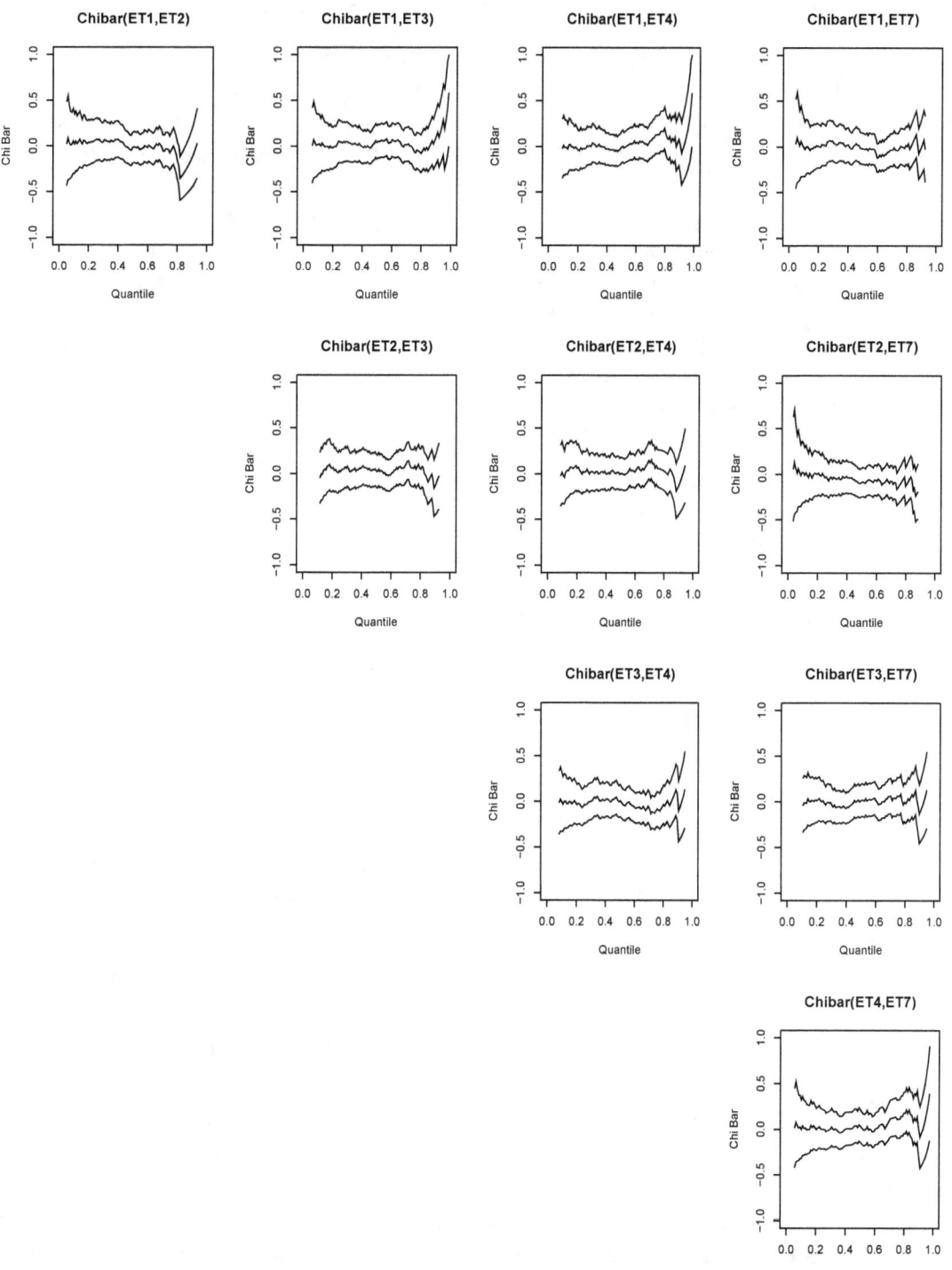

Figure 16: Dependence Structure at Various Quantiles, outliers excluded

4.4 Bodies, Tails, and Separate Treatment of Outliers

Excluding the outliers only affects our maximum likelihood estimates modestly, but has significant effects on the estimated capital charge. The correlation tests for raw data with excluded outliers are reported in Table 3. Interestingly, the removal of four weeks that contained outliers eliminated most pairwise correlations between weekly losses of various event types, with the exception of the Pearson correlation between Events 4 and 7 which becomes significant at the 10% level after elimination of the outliers. For this particular data set, that would suggest that analysis of the data without the outliers may be conducted under the assumption of uncorrelatedness. The reverse side of this coin is that the separate scenario analysis of the outliers would require careful calibration of correlatedness, both in data analysis, and when eliciting priors from experts. However, hasty generalization from the specifics of one bank's data set is not warranted. Hence, one should allow for correlatedness of the bodies and tails of distributions – using copula as we do in this paper, or using some other statistical methodology – and also allow for correlatedness of extremely infrequent and large events, which we call outliers. If no correlation exists, then allowing for it will not affect the analysis adversely, but the reverse is not true, since diversification effects can be significant as we show in the conclusion.

Table 3: Pearson's Product-moment Correlations and Tests of Uncorrelatedness – raw data without outliers

Event Types	Pearson Corr.	t-statistic	d.f.	p-value
E1, E2	-0.054	-0.747	190	0.456
E1, E3	-0.012	-0.162	190	0.872
E1, E4	-0.026	-0.353	190	0.872
E1, E7	-0.021	-0.293	190	0.770
E2, E3	-0.008	-0.114	190	0.910
E2, E4	0.060	-0.082	190	0.406
E2, E7	-0.019	-0.263	190	0.793
E3, E4	-0.042	-0.579	190	0.563
E3, E7	0.048	0.658	190	0.511
E4, E7	0.125	1.741	190	0.03

The estimated lognormal parameters for types 1 and 3 are only affected in the second decimal place. The new estimates of bodies and tails for types 2, 4, and 7 are shown in Figures 17, 18, and 19, respectively. The main effects are that the threshold quantile is lower for event type 4 and higher for 7, and the shape parameter for event type 4 tail GPD is significantly lower. The latter effect is primarily responsible for the different capital charge that we estimate with this model.

28

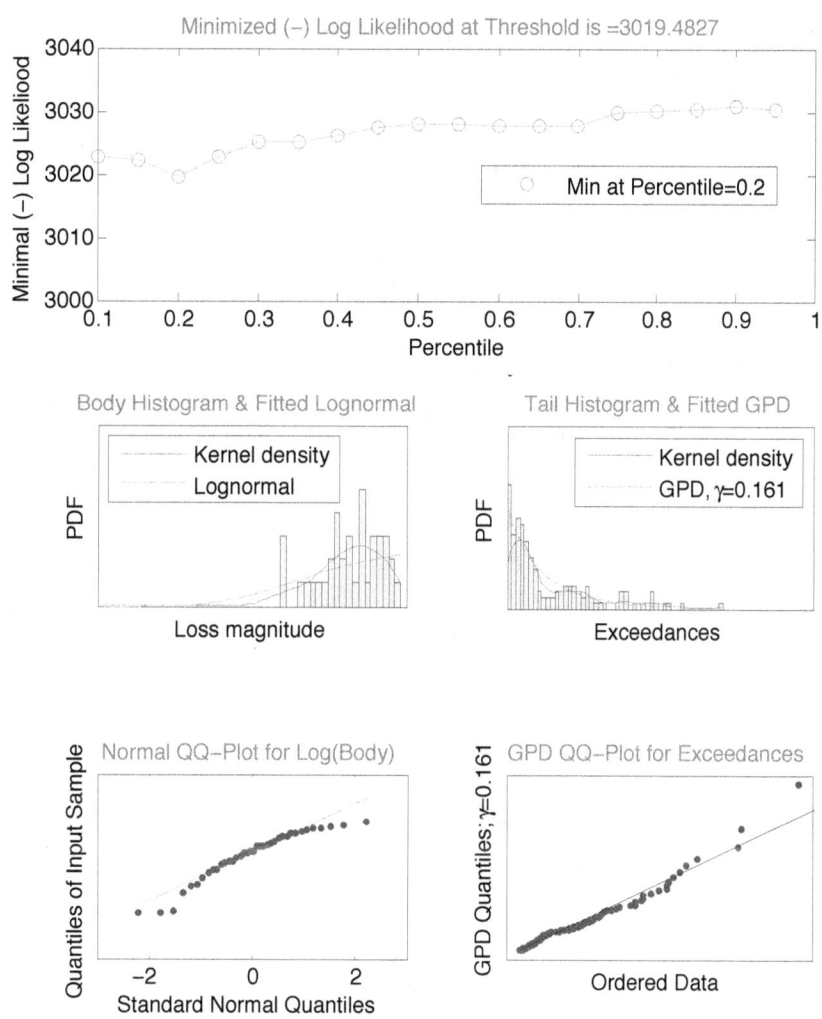

Figure 17: Lognormal Body & GPD Tail Fit for Event Type 2, Outliers Excluded

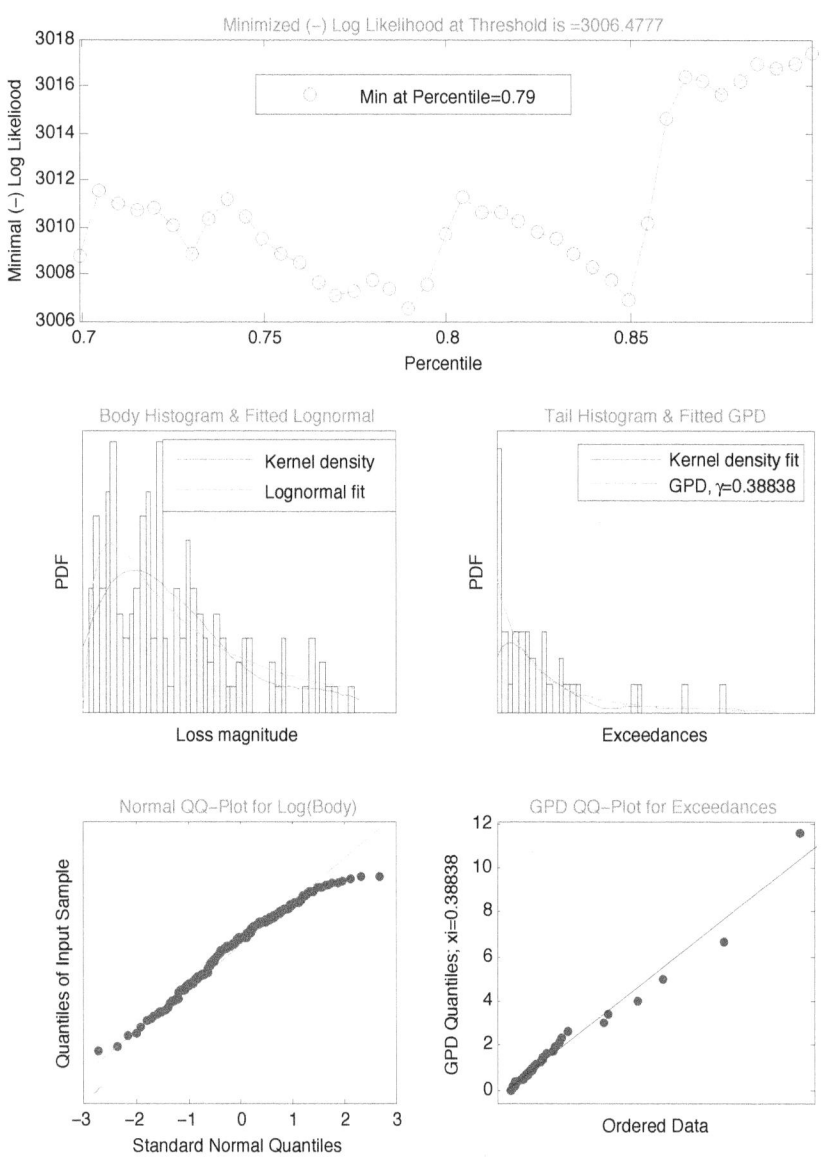

Figure 18: Lognormal Body & GPD Tail Fit for Event Type 4, Outliers Excluded

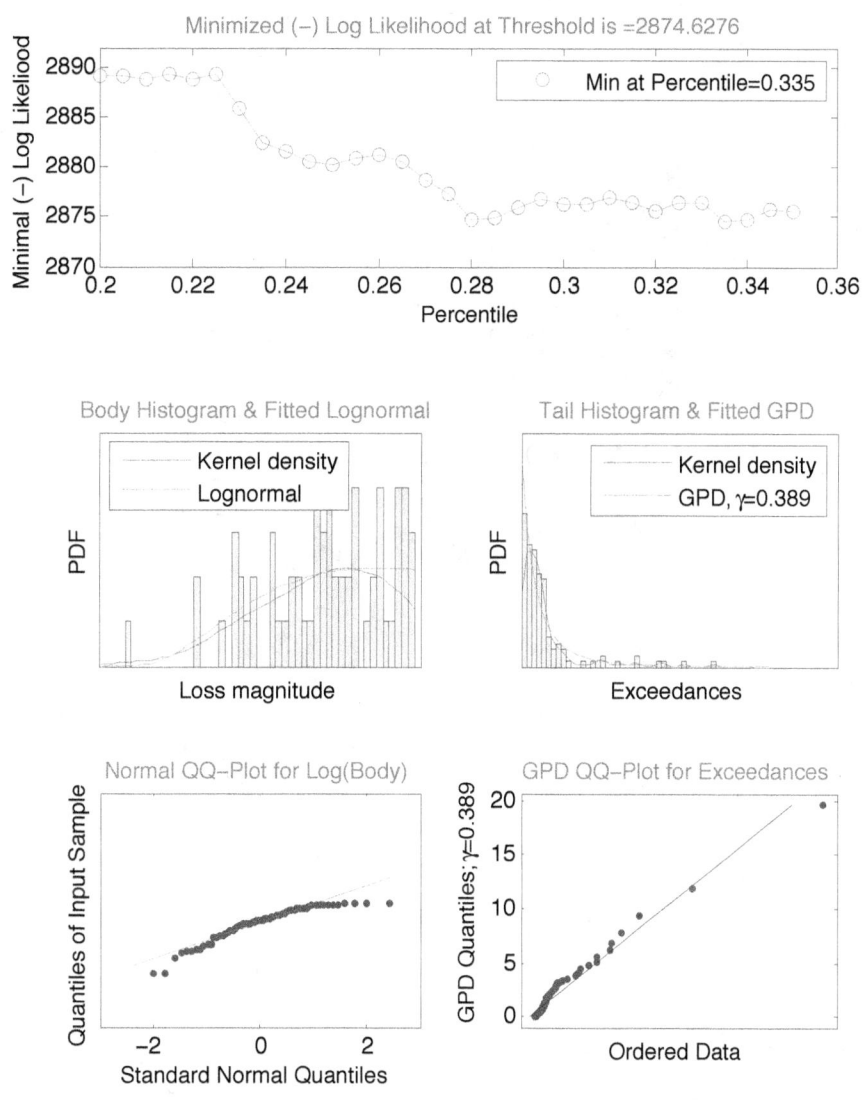

Figure 19: Lognormal Body & GPD Tail Fit for Event Type 7, Outliers Excluded

31

As we can see in Figure 20, the Spearman correlations estimated with this model (using EVT, but excluding outliers for future probabilistic scenario analysis) differ from previous estimates in significant ways. Most notable is the high Spearman correlation between event types 4 and 7, which is higher than those observed in either of the previous models.

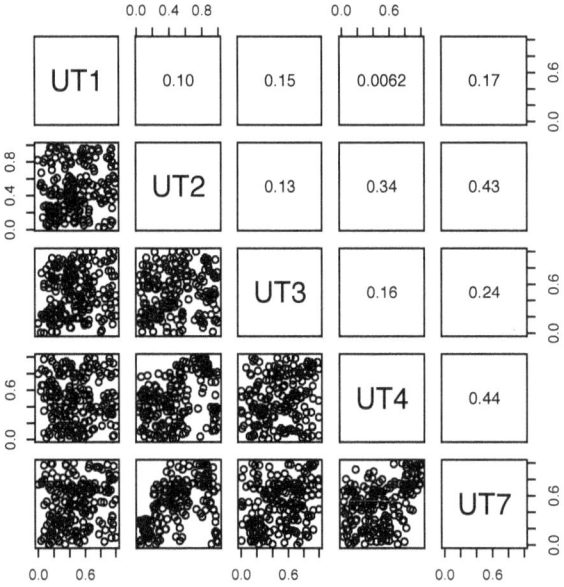

Figure 20: Scatterplot: Lognormal Bodies & GPD Tails, Outliers Excluded

The elimination of outliers also has the effect of moderating quantiles of the estimated distribution of annual operational losses. Figure 21 shows that simulated distribution based on the estimated weekly marginals and t-copula after the four outlier weeks were excluded. Recall that the simulated annual losses were normalized so that the internal estimate of $VaR_{99.9\%}$ for this bank was \$1 billion. The hybrid model, which incorporates EVT but excluded outliers, produces an estimated $VaR_{99.9\%}$ of \$551 million, which leaves a reasonable cushion for probabilistic scenario analysis of extremely rare and extremely large outliers. The results of our three models are thus summarized in Table 4.

4.4.1 Adjusting VaR for outliers

Of course, when we exclude outliers from our main statistical analysis, we must perform a separate statistical analysis of the outlier generation process, and the distribution of outliers conditional on their occurrence. Due to the rareness of outliers, it is ideal to use a Bayesian analysis, with priors on occurrence, severity, and co-dependence of outliers elicited from experts at the relevant banks. The full treatment of this procedure is a subject for future research. A back of the envelope calculation using only the observations we have would suggest an adjustment to the VaR that is of an appropriate magnitude. With outliers

Table 4: Value at Risks and Expected Shortfalls (in $ US billions, using copula)

Model	VaR$_{95\%}$	VaR$_{99\%}$	VaR$_{99.9\%}$	ES$_{95\%}$	ES$_{99\%}$	ES$_{99.9\%}$
All data, lognormal only	0.160	0.208	0.327	0.192	0.259	0.424
All data, with EVT	2.795	6.561	28.407	7.478	21.855	119.330
Without 3 outliers, with EVT	0.481	0.731	1.721	0.678	1.148	2.869
Without 4 outliers, with EVT	0.283	0.354	0.551	0.335	0.442	0.763
Without 5 outliers, with EVT	0.230	0.271	0.367	0.258	0.312	0.461

observed in four weeks out of a sample of 194, and assuming that the weekly probability of observing one or more outliers is independent across weeks, we may assume that the weekly process is Poisson with mean $\lambda = 4/194 = 0.02$.

In a full analysis, we would generate our simulated weekly samples by first using i.i.d. Poisson draws to determine whether the week is an outlier or a regular week, and then drawing from the appropriate distribution conditional on that draw. For the current back of the envelope calculation, we may assume that we draw exactly one outlier week in a year ($4 \times 52/194 = 1.072 \approx 1$). To simulate a distribution of outlier severity conditional on occurrence, we cannot rely on observed data alone, due to their very small number. Hence, we would have to elicit priors from experts and to perform a Bayesian analysis based on those priors and observed data. For our back of the envelope combination, we may simply take the largest observed loss in the four observed weeks out of 194 as an underestimate proxy for the high percentile that we would use in calculating overall VaR (the high percentile will usually fall outside the support of observed data). Scaling our largest week's total loss by the same factor that we have used in this paper, we get $133.9 million, which would bring the overall VaR value to $684 million, which is of the order of magnitude that we would expect, given our use of an underestimate of an extreme tail percentile using an observed datum. Of course, in the full analysis, we would also simulate the outliers by event type, allowing for various types of correlations as elicited from experts, and extrapolating beyond the sample using estimated tail distribution parameters. However, for the purposes of this paper, the back-of-the-envelope calculation in this subsection illustrates the order of magnitude addition to the capital charge that we would expect, once we integrate a Bayesian-scenario analysis of outliers with the rest of our statistical analysis.

4.5 Summary of Results

The results in Table 4 provide us with a clear prescription: Ignoring EVT analysis entirely would produce erroneously low capital charges, while using EVT indiscriminately would produce excessively large ones. The correct approach appears to be using EVT judiciously;

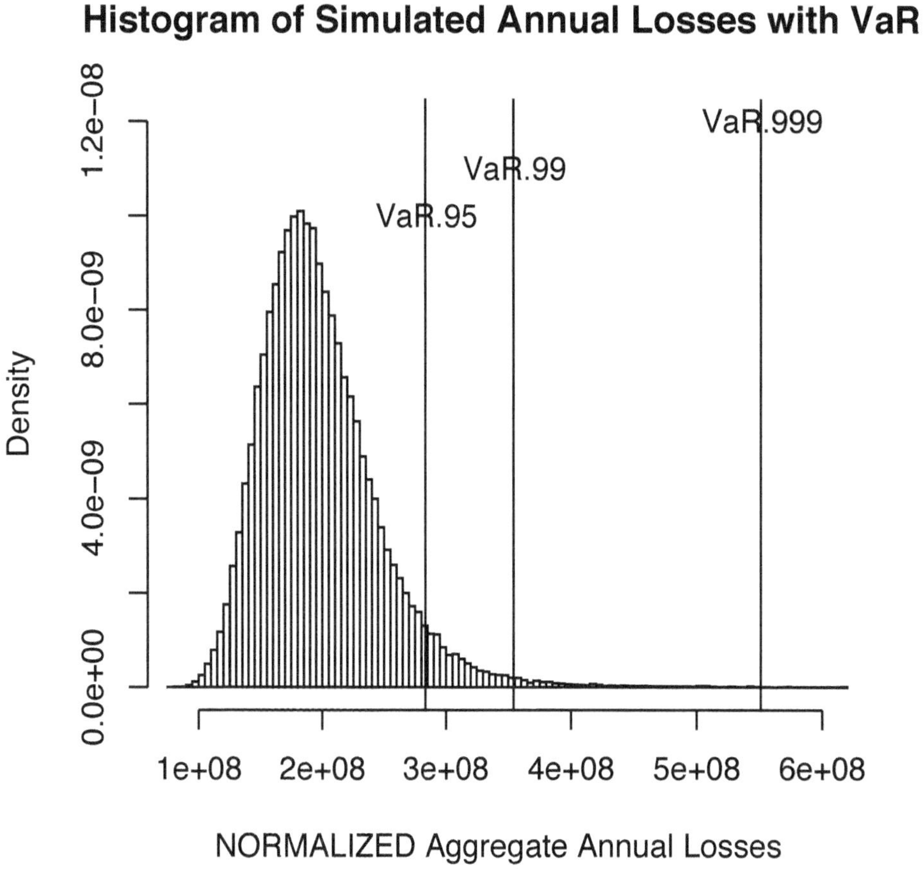

Histogram of Simulated Annual Losses with VaR

Figure 21: The Bottom Line: Lognormal Bodies, GPD Tails, & Excluded Outliers

only if dictated by the likelihood function, and only after extremely large and rare outliers are excluded. The capital charge obtained from that analysis must then be complemented with a probabilistic scenario analysis for outliers.

One final analysis must be conducted before we conclude the paper. Some banks have argued that allowing for less-than-perfect correlations between loss types, as we have done in our analysis, can result in "diversification effects" that are as high as 20–70%. This diversification effect is the difference between the estimated capital charge assuming perfect correlation between event types (i.e. adding up the 99.9th percentiles for each loss type to obtain the capital charge), as opposed to using simulations with estimated copula based on Spearman correlation coefficients.

In Table 5, we report the VaR values that we would have obtained in Table 4 had we assumed perfect correlation. The range of diversification effects suggested by our calculations is 0.5–10.7%. This number may become higher once we allow for diversification effects across rare but extreme outliers, but remains unlikely to reach the range above 20%. Hence, our analysis suggests that regulators should be receptive to the idea of diversifi-

34

cation effects reducing the required capital charge, but should remain skeptical regarding unreasonably large estimates of those effects.

Table 5: VaRs assuming perfect correlation + Diversification Effect for VaR$_{99.9\%}$

Model	VaR$_{95\%}$	VaR$_{99\%}$	VaR$_{99.9\%}$	diversification effect
All data, lognormal only	0.173	0.225	0.362	10.7%
All data, with EVT	2.783	6.859	28.535	0.5%
Without 3 outliers, with EVT	0.492	0.752	1.761	2.3%
Without 4 outliers, with EVT	0.293	0.372	0.590	7.1%
Without 5 outliers, with EVT	0.240	0.289	0.399	8.9%

5 Concluding Remarks

Despite the Basel Committee's explicit emphasis on conducting operational risk quantification and management analysis at the most appropriately disaggregated level possible, most banks have been pooling all operational losses and calculating capital charges based on univariate estimation of the loss distribution. Alternatively, some other banks have argued for "diversification benefits," seeking to reduce their operational risk capital charges based on ad hoc assumptions about correlations between different types of operational losses.

In this regard, [17] reported that:

> Most of the AMA framework institutions adjusted their AMA capital for diversification. About half of the institutions stated their correlation assumptions, while some estimated only one loss distribution at the firm-wide level, thus implying a zero correlation assumption. Institutions did not provide empirical support for their chosen diversification/correlation assumptions, as correlation assumptions relied primarily on expert judgment. Potentially, these correlation/diversification assumptions could have a significant impact in the risk exposure calculations.

In this paper, we have proposed a sophisticated and yet easy-to-implement approach to utilizing state-of-the-art risk-estimation methodologies utilizing maximum likelihood copula estimation. Together with careful univariate maximum likelihood estimation, and allowing for judicious use of extreme value theory methods where appropriate, we have shown how "diversification benefits" can be estimated coherently. The resulting range of those benefits (as percentages of the capital charge equal to value at risk at the 99.9% level) is significant, but smaller than the range commonly proposed by banks.

Our multivariate statistical approach follows the spirit of the Basel II Accord by dividing observed losses in each category into regular losses, extreme losses, and outliers. The maximum likelihood approach to estimating univariate distributions for regular and extreme losses (where appropriate), as well as copula for modeling the dependence structure for those losses, easily scales to larger numbers of loss categories within the operational risk framework, and can potentially be extended to modeling credit and market risks. In other words, the general approach is sufficiently flexible to consider "diversification benefits" not only within operational risk categories, but also between operational risk and other forms of banking risk.

Moreover, the likelihood-based approach lends itself easily to Bayesian analysis (imposing prior distributions on model parameters and using the maximum likelihood estimates to seed efficient Gibbs sampling). In turn, this makes it easy to integrate this analysis with probabilistic scenario analyses of very rare and very large losses, as proposed for example by [15, 16]. Eventually, integrating those methods can assist in building a coherent and comprehensive statistical model for bank risk quantification and management.

Table 6: Synchronizing Operational Losses: Illustration of Aggregation of Losses for ET4 and ET7

Days	ET4	ET7	Weeks	ET4	ET7
d_1	n.a.	$L7_1$	w_1	$AL4_1$	$AL7_1$
d_2	n.a.	$L7_{2,1}, L7_{2,2}$	w_2	$AL4_2$	$AL7_2$
.	.	.	.	.	.
d_k	$L4_k$	$L7_k$	w_k	$AL4_k$	$AL7_k$
.	.	.	.	.	.
d_{365}	n.a.	$L7_n$	w_{52}	$AL4_n$	$AL7_n$

Table 7: Number of excesses used in EVT analysis when threshold estimated by MLE

ETs	All Data	Without 3 Outliers	Without 4 Outliers	Without 5 Outliers
ET2	157	154	154	153
ET4	32	41	40	39
ET7	141	139	128	137

Figure 22: Box plot to identify outliers for each ET

References

[1] Beirlant, J., Y. Goegebeur, J. Teugels and J. Teugels, (2004), *Statistics of Extremes: Theory and Applications*, NY: Wiley.

[2] Cibele, N. B., H. F. Lopes, and D. Gamerman, (2004), "Bayesian analysis of extreme events with threshold estimation," *Statistical Modelling*, Volume 4, Number 3, October, pp. 227–244.

[3] Coles, S., (2001), *An introduction to statistical modeling of extreme values*, London: Springer-Verlag.

[4] Coles, S. G., J. Heffernan, and J. A. Tawn, (1999), "Dependence measures for multivariate extremes," *Extremes*, 2, pp. 339–365.

[5] Danielsson, J., L. de Haan, L. Peng, and C. G. de Vries, (2001), "Using a bootstrap method to choose the sample fraction in tail index estimation," *Journal of Multivariate Analysis*, 76, pp. 226–248.

[6] de Fontnouvelle, P., J.S. Jordan, and E.S. Rosengren, (2005), "Implications of alternative operational risk modeling techniques," NBER Working Paper No. 11103.

[7] de Fontnouvelle, P., V. Garrity, S. Chu, and E. Rosengren, (2005), "The Potential Impact of Explicit Basel II Operational Risk Capital Charges on the Competitive Environment of Processing Banks in the United States," Working Paper, Federal Reserve Bank of Boston.

[8] Demarta, S. and A.J. McNeil, (2004), "The t copula and related copulas," ETH Working Paper.

[9] Di Clemente, A., and Romano, R, (2004), "A copula-extreme value theory approach for modeling operational risk," in *Operational risk Modelling Analysis*, Edited by Marcelo Cruz, London: Risk Books.

[10] Dutta, K., and J. Perry, (2006), "A Tale of Tails: An Empirical Analysis of Loss Distribution Models for Estimating Operational Risk Capital," Working Paper, Federal Reserve Bank of Boston.

[11] Embrechts, P., C. Kluppelberg, and T. Mikosch, (1997), *Modeling Extremal Events for Insurance and Finance*, Berlin, Germany: Springer-Verlag.

[12] Embrechts, P., McNeil, A.J. and D. Straumann (2002), Correlation and dependency in risk management properties and pitfalls, in *Risk Management: Value at Risk and Beyond*, ed. M.A.H. Dempster, Cambridge: Cambridge University Press.

[13] Frachot, A., Roncalli, T., and Salomon, E., (2005), "Correlation and diversification effects in operational risk modeling,"in *Operational Risk: Practical approaches to implementation*, Edited By Ellen Davis, London: Risk Books.

[14] Johnson, N.L., S. Kotz and N. Balakrishnan (1997), *Discrete Multivariate Distributions*, Wiley Series in Probability and Statistics, NY: John Wiley & Sons.

[15] Kiefer, N.M., (2006a), "Default estimation for low-default portfolios,"OCC Working Paper.

[16] Kiefer, N.M., (2006b), "The probability approach to default probabilities,"OCC Working Paper.

[17] LDCE (2005), Results of the 2004 Loss Data Collection Exercise for Operational Risk, at http://www.bos.frb.org/bankinfo/qau/pd051205.pdf

[18] McNeil, A., R. Frey, and P. Embrechts, (2005), *Quantitative Risk Management*, NJ: Princeton University Press.

[19] Powojowski, M.R., D. Reynolds and H.J.H. Tuenter, (2002) "Dependent Events and Operational Risk," Algo Research Quarterly, 5(2), pp. 65–73.

[20] Risk Management Group, (2003), The 2002 Loss Data Collection Exercise for Operational Risk: Summary of the Data Collected, Report to Basel Committee on Banking Supervision, Bank for International Settlements.

[21] Sklar, A., (1959), "Fonctions de repartition a n dimensions et leurs marges, *Publications de l'Institut de Statistique de l'Universite de Paris*, 8, pp. 229–231.